Thoughts on the Scientific State

Anarcho-syndicalism and Social Ecology in a World Set Free: New Keynesian Thought and the Scientific Order

By

Miguel A. Sanchez-Rey

Table of Contents

Introduction

The political economy of the state is in principled the management of the means of production. Control of the means of production protects the populace from the tyranny of both private markets and private interests. In that manner Karl Marx envisioned that state-capitalism will by revolutionary means lead to the proletariat state. A state that eventually gradually dissolves into anarchy.

It isn't clear how the dismantling of the state is to lead to anarchism, both to Karl Marx and Friedrich Engels, but various power arrangements are conjectured as to the role of government and how the means of production is to be organized in an anarchist society.

When certain power arrangements are no longer necessary and in which those power arrangements can be counter-productive those arrangements are to be torn down in favor of democratic control [whether by councils or unions]. [1] The state exists to protect the interests of the populace and the political economy of state protects those interests by meeting their needs and by which those needs are properly objectified.

It's then the Scientific State is to arise from the hostility between the corporate state and the democratic state. The Scientific State, being the logical and consistent, extension of workers trade groups and market interests can be said to be an ecological planetary society that very much resembles a centralized state but in which centralized power is self-regulatory and in which the population plays no part in the decisions of the state -- means of production and in which governing of industry is to be democratically self-manage and in no purview to the motives of the state.

The existentiality of the Scientific State is grounded on the policy of social ecology and New Keynesian principles that are not antithetical to workers councils and trade groups. [2] Those policies of ecological flight fuels and gives life to the state in which care of the state can avoid disintegration and entropy.

Here the Scientific Order is explain and in which this order can be enacted without violent struggle. The Scientific Age is in many ways the sign of the beginning of a new democratic order. The affairs of the state, being tantamount and dependent on technological progress, is the purview of a select body [a council of administrators and architects] and in which that select body can take control of the Scientific Age. Progress of innovation and commerce, trade groups and markets, are regulated by individual initiative and in which the accumulation of wealth is no longer the guiding protocol of the Scientific State rather progress in technology and economic growth.

Regulation of commerce and trade in which a central institution controls the flow of wealth and solvency of debt is the guiding force of New Keynesian economics [3]. Here the regulatory body sees fit to take action, when necessary, to prevent the slow-down of the national or international of economy and to avoid hyperinflation.

John Maynard Keynes set to overcome the limits of communist ideology [4]. Having addressed the problematics of classical economics Lord Keynes established demand/supply side economics [3]. The bedrock of which the government is to take action when there is the recession is the midst of an economic slow-down or crises. The modern Keynesian approach stipulates that a regulatory body is to control the accumulation of wealth and see fit that when the accumulation of debt is necessary and when inflation should be avoided when debt is too burdernsome.

Here the Scientific State is to take an independent role from the affairs of commercial and market interests. But in which those interests of necessity and privatization does not interfere with regulation. Trade groups and democratic control of the means of production is still subject to New Keynesian. As the federalization of democratic industry, and the elimination of state-government, must then be regulated by the commerce of exchange of innovation and technological applications of scientific advances.

When technological and scientific advances are achieved the exchange of economic needs and wants is not immune to an economic slow-down or hyper-growth. With secular stagnation permanent recession means the continual stimulation of the industry of trade groups helps to avoid a slow-down of technological progress while exchange of technology, by which stimulation of both commerce and buying power, helps to preserve the federation of diverse industrial bodies [5]. Individualized industrial needs are met by a centralized regulatory entity. An independent entity that overrides self-interests but in which long-term self-interests can be beneficial and productive.

The reality of New Keynesian demand/supply side economics and in which government is to take a pro-active stance in the preservation of both individual and collective well-being and both self and collective actualization [4]. Without which conflict is to arise and the Scientific State is threaten.

The Scientific State existence, nevertheless, is attached to the independence of regulatory banking. But the state is not to interfere in the affairs of commercial and private interests. Private interests and commercial needs are to be control by trade regulation and the solvency of the flow of debt and the accumulation of overall economic wealth.

Workers councils and the democratic decision making of production is the most logical step in an advance industrial society [6]. As classical liberalism has stated that the artistic drive for creativity and productivity is both a necessary component of individual well-being and a necessary means in which an individual views labor as a free enterprise of creative action and fulfillment [7].

The means of production, whereby, self-interest is the guiding architecture and in which collective responsibility is a measure of internal and external long-terms profits. The Scientific State, both independent of economic uncertainties and dependent on the vitality of commerce, views self-management to be an imminent drive. In which if self-management is not a preclusion of state interest opposition to the state would be inevitable as individuals cannot achieve self-actualization and mental well-being is threatened by the tyranny of state sovereignty.

Individual action to take part in the industrial process achieves self-interest and a guiding force for collective action and protectionism. The Scientific State, if whether or not possible, is to keep its reach off the self-management of the means of the production. That the populace forbid itself from the interest of the reigning government. That the administration of political economy be overseen by democratic self-management and that such self-management is tantamount to technological progress and the accomplishment of innovation.

Different specialized industrial sectors look after the interests of its workforce and that its workforce not be deprived of the benefits of exchange and buying power. That each and every other being achieve its own desires and interests while protecting and achieving the overall certainty of the fulfillment of labor and ideals. Though the realism of economic and political forces not be excluded from the decisions of political economy.

The Council of the Scientific State

The socialist state, in which Karl Marx envisioned, is very much, like a capitalist state, a prison to the individual in need [7]. There is never the negligence, in the Scientific State, that a beings well-being be protected and that the defense of the state be considered far more than the affairs of production and labor. The council, ever more sophisticated and a necessary evil, mandate is to oversee the protection of the individual from harm; both technological and militaristic. A semi-pacifist state the council of the Scientific State, or a planetary state, achieves a serene society by excluding knowledge of external and internal threats from public consciousness.

In doing so the democratic system is protected from internal strife and the panic of existential futility. Otherwise the overthrow of the Scientific State could cause havoc and the technological and industrial achievements leads only to implosion and self-destruction. Auto-immunity subsist and democratic order collapses to the detriment of the Scientific Age [8].

Surmounting only to chaotic rule and dynamical instability of economic policy. The Council of the Scientific State must see to protect the populace from panic and to take whatever action is necessary to preserve order and tranquility.

A body politic, nevertheless, but a political necessity to the state and abolishment of centralized power structures and tyranny. Whom makes the ultimate decision in the affairs of the state, and in which, deadlock is avoided, is by override and by careful logical analysis of any decision for military action and humanitarian intervention.

The Scientific Age

An age of scientific progress and innovation. Where the population is periodically shut out of the scientific process to protect them from any breakdown in the sciences. How such declaration to manage the Scientific Age and to prevent knowledge of such an age from leaking into mainstream consciousness, and that the wild ideas of the Scientific Age be controlled is to be enacted by the policy changes in academia and the state laboratories. Policy decisions that consist of a lockdown in high level academic research, higher academic standards that selects individuals to participate in the Scientific Age and limits in the duration/substance of tenure in the state laboratories.

Design to achieve a more vibrant and technological society the payoffs of limitations to the participation of decision-making processes of the scientific endeavor is ever an age of wild-anticipation. Social and technological progress must await as the scientific process is undergoing and when such knowledge is gradually and periodically disclose the public consciousness in neither startled nor giving in to a flight or fight response.

The participants of the Scientific Age carries the burden of contributing immensely to innovation and technological progress but when they are cut off from the scientific process they must condition themselves to the torment and grief of non-participation and to await the success of their own contributions to scientific research. A global effort the achievements of the Scientific Age, by cutting off the general public from the scientific process, leads to a sustainable existence. Public consciousness and excitement sustains the scientific process while protecting the scientific process from internal and external strife. Avoiding a breakdown in the sciences; protecting the Scientific State from democratic collapse by rational auto-immunity.

Environmental life, and the ecological threats posed by careless industrialization, raises ethical questions' about the organization of social life [2]. It's known that individual consciousness is very much dependent on environmental factors. By organizing social life base on preserving the health of the environment and preservation of biodiversity the planetary scientific state achieves a change in the outlook of private interests and the individual and collective admission that the state must protect the environment. Yet the state council, ever more a distant force, individual communes guide themselves on the dynamics of the environment and the progress of technology. The more progress in technology, in the field of medicine, chemistry and physics, the more likely the sustainability of economic growth and environmental recovery.

Eventually expansion from a planetary body preserves the survival of the species and lowers population growth. Protecting the environment from a population explosion and any other internal/external threats dealt by any foreseeable scenario in which long-term species survival is threatened.

Ethical considerations of controlling the environment on a planetary scale and policies which limit the exploitation of the environment is a scientific matter. Yet the planetary state must be aware of the misuse of the environment on a technological scale. Market interests, as well, must adhere to limits in consumption and consumerism. Whereby interests in material gains can preserve mental well-being while protecting the environment from exploitation.

Even with environmental technological progress the development of new habitats outside the planetary body is necessary if equilibrium is to be achieved and resistance to ever greater control of environmental policy can be mitigated.

The New Scientific Order: Dictatorship and Democratic Control

Current political strife has eluded to the rise of a scientific dictatorship. In which the democratic order has shifted away from parliamentary decision making and checks and balances between representational government and executive power. As such national decision-making has become more centralized.

The corporate-capitalist drive for control of markets and short-term profits has fed into economic instability while mass insurrection has turned the public consciousness away from regulatory over-sight. Though economic growth has persisted since the last economic crises of 2008-2012; the lasting damage to public democratic ownership of parliamentary and representative government, the corporate take-over of the Supreme Court in United States, has hinted that executive action, in the form of the executive order, can bypass the representative and parliamentary system toward centralized rule of law.

A scientific dictatorship in which the central government has total control of the population and yet the needs of the population are met; whereby well-being is achieved at a large-scale and that defense of the state is tantamount, is a haunting image of the limits of current democracy. The state machine and military machine is a tyrannical object. When such machines are allowed to get out of control, whereby, public protest against such entities is crushed, and in that private markets take over the management of the state, a scientific dictatorship is the only political economy that can preserve the tranquility of the populace while safe-guarding capitalist interest and preventing mass opposition toward the establishment.

The Defense of the Scientific State from Catastrophe

The prevention of a foreseeable catastrophic scenario in the Scientific Age is the first step toward a defense of the Scientific State. The other goal of defending the Scientific State is to protect the tranquility of the state both by enforcing military and humanitarian intervention. Though the council has utmost control of such military force it's to be guided by individual rights; both natural and civil.

Economic interests and political needs are not to use such military forces to quash public protest but to protect the public from external threats. The dismantling of military forces is to be decided when the Scientific State is being carried away; and only then do we realize that the Scientific Age has grown up. By then anarchy has been achieved.

Conclusion: The New International

Variation of ideas in a diverse planetary scientific society in which devotion to the welfare of each being is structured on the unification of economic interests by free-trade and globalization of market forces. There are opposition to such evolutionary socialist ideals but in all such opposition is a natural process of liberalization and civilization of isolated pockets of primitive societies and industrialization. Though the modern world has yet to realize a sustainable and tranquil existence it's expected that such accomplishment is not too far away but it is an arduous step that requires political and economic action.

Technological advances is only one avenue in achieving a world set free from the bondage to capitalist classical economics and corporate tyranny. The state exist to protect the populace from private power and interests. As such the Scientific State exists to protect the populace from breaks down in the democratic process, both in the Scientific Age and by external/internal threats, that pose existential risks to tranquil life.

The population remains independently self-existent. The decisions they make, both in short term and long-term, are there's to make while the decisions of the Scientific State are there to prevent catastrophe and uncertainty in long-term species survival. Negligence toward well-being of individuals is an intolerable trait to planetary society. The desire for selfish self-interests must be tempered by the jurisprudence of consequences in the Scientific Age. All beings desire to achieve and actualize as to protect psychological health; and in doing so free-markets and integration of independent markets toward a federalized industrial society is the most rational course while the Scientific State is inevitable outcome.

References

[1] Rocker, Rudolf. *Anarcho-Syndicalism*. Phoenix Press.

[2] Purchase, Graham. *Anarchism and Ecology.* Black Rose Books: 1997.

[3] Keynes, John Maynard. *The General Theory of Employment, Interests, and Money.* Classics Unbound.

[4] Keynes, John Maynard. *Essays in Persuasion.* W.W. Norton and Company: 1963.

[5] Guerin, Daniel. *Anarchism.* Monthly Review Press: 1970.

[6] Chomsky, Noam. *Government in the Future.* Seven Stories Press: 1970.

[7] Von Humboldt, Wilhelm. *The Limits of State Action.*

[8] Derrida, Jacques. *Rogues.* Stanford University Press: 2005.

PHPR

By

Miguel A. Sanchez-Rey

Government is a resolution to the state-of-nature [1]. The Physicalist Program [PHPR] is design as a resolution to a foreseeable catastrophic scenario in the Scientific Age in the form of a task. The Grandmaster is to complete a task and set the next task.

The First Task of PHPR is a 100 Year Task [2].

When the International Thermonuclear Experimental Reactor [ITER] goes online the planetary system will begin to gradually recover. A 40 year period of sustainable economic growth and environmental recovery sets a window of opportunity to complete 60 percent of the First Task of PHPR. After which there will be a global decline when ITER is off the manufacturing line.

PHPR is to be dismantled when the last task is completed. By then the Scientific Age has come to an end...

References

[1] Hobbes, Thomas. Leviathan. Oxford University Press: 1996.

[2] Sanchez-Rey, Miguel A. The Physicalist Program. Createspace: 2015.

The Scientific Age

By,

Miguel A. Sanchez-Rey

Post-Modernity is a tragedy of ideology and thought. Ideology which is both speechless and thoughtless. A speechless and thoughtless theatre of anguish pride and pretentious regret. But if prideful regret is both speechless and thoughtless; then, it is a speechless thought. A window of loss opportunity to a schizophrenic cause that knows no limits.

Since the end of modernity there had been conscientious fear and loathing of the scientific machine. A machine which is a brutal byproduct of social Darwinist extremism and the fantasy driven radicalism of anarcho-capitalism. A machine which is a corporate state that guides itself on sadomasochism and control.

Reactionaries [the counter-Enlightens and the theorists in criticality] set to perform an anatomical study of how such a machine could have arisen from the ashes of war and peace. What they learned is that the desperation of those of economical need fueled the rise of criminal elements which fulfilled their thirst and mania. Criminal elements that only too soon ravished their thoughtless regret into political genocide and racial grief.

After which the fall of the scientific machine led to beginning of the modern democratic state in the form of a controlled Keynesian economy call state-capitalism. For nearly 20 years, after the world-wide implementation of Keynesian thought, the community of nations experienced an economic boom as more and more power was giving to the state to regulate and control the excesses of profits and private industry.

Whispers could be heard along the offices of the intelligentsia and academic establishment of brave impotence and extravagance. They gathered together in book stores and coffee houses as debating bodies. They travelled long distances to give talks. They had established the modern democratic academy of thought.

The modern democracy of thought fought against the criminalization of dangerous ideas. They had set the stage for equality and rights of different races and ethnicity. They had become an outgrowth of the falling societies of those before then whom had cried bitterly to voice their neglect and blind oppression.

It's then that the public and intelligentsia had reached the dawned of Post-Modernity. Wishful thinkers of a braver scientism that is both unreasonable and uncontrollably creative. They set their heights too far; braver than the thinkers' of the Enlightens, but they were grounded by their hopes of a lasting end to their marginalization in artistic technocratic expressionism.

The new democratic establishment opened the doors to free-thinking and education. Education became a force for both civilizing their constituents and controlling their primitive habits. Their wild contemplation became a spirit to partake in the democratic process; leading only to free-markets and neo-liberalism. The New Left had falling and then arose the modern American and European establishment. An establishment in which control of markets had been transferred to private interest, education had become a universal right and entertainment and sports led the way to a complacent consumerist population.

The modern world finally crash as war and sociopathic behavior became the norm. A norm that very much resembles a newer type of organized crime. A crime of extreme academia and extreme economy; the bitterness of others whom could not participate in the technocratic state. They despised their degradation but their motivation is a brutal realism.

The scientific establishment, ever more worrisome and troubled, saw a democratic society in which the mass information and mass communication fed into the fantasies of paranoia and conspiracy. Scientific research, scientific advances, big new science, and all things scientism were reactions to a confuse sense of globalizations failure to integrate with modern ideas and social progress. Religious extremism and militism wrongly became a force for good while technology and scientific advances became an impediment to free thought and self-determination.

At the very edge victims of a scientific machine unlike before. A machine that aroused fantasy and flattery. Mutilated by the desire for collective over-achievement while neglecting the consequences of over-extending the bounds of intelligence. We have then until now reach the Scientific Age.

It's in this age that contemplation of the scientific process becomes limited in that the general establishment and the public must forgo decision-making in the sciences. The sciences are ever more motivated to enact extreme ideals and fantasies as to realize a world set free from the shackles of barbarism and conflict. To continue to allow public thought to partake in the sciences without boundaries risks to reward bad-decision making and to wrongly exclude others from participating. How far should the limits of scientific participation go and how then should the populace live their lives if not to be tormented by the unforeseeable and unknowable?

It's a strong age of wild anticipation but also sacrifice as to protect the scientific state from democratic collapse. Some wild thoughts are productive and some are not. Wild thoughts are ever more the driving force of the Scientific Age but nevertheless tempered by scientific jurisprudence, and duty to the scientific method and inquiry.

Is this the fruition of a scientific dictatorship some would ask? A change of the democratic order in the region of experimentation and theory? What responsibilities does the field of ethics hold to the values of logic?

Periodically and gradually does knowledge of the Scientific Age become known but only little by little does one know more and more. Technological progress and innovation becomes the goal of the Scientific Age as a vibrant society becomes more and more visible to sight, touch and sound. It's a serene and quiet time of utmost strength as the radicalism and extremism of Post-Modernity is ever more a haunting lesson of prideful regret.